WHAT SHALL COME HEREAFTER

The Afterworld: What I Wish I'd Known

D'Anne Olsen, Ph.D.

What Shall Come Hereafter: The Afterworld, What I Wish I'd Known. Copyright ©2019 D'Anne Olsen, Ph.D. Produced and printed by Stillwater River Publications. All rights reserved. Written and produced in the United States of America. This book may not be reproduced or sold in any form without the expressed, written permission of the author and publisher.

Visit our website at www.StillwaterPress.com for more information.

First Stillwater River Publications Edition

ISBN-13: 978-1-950339-15-0
ISBN-10: 1-950339-15-7

12345678910

Written by D'Anne Olsen, Ph.D.
Published by Stillwater River Publications, Pawtucket, RI 02860

Publisher's Cataloging-In-Publication Data
(Prepared by The Donohue Group, Inc.)

Names: Olsen, D'Anne, author.
Title: What shall come hereafter : the Afterworld : what I wish I'd known / D'Anne Olsen, Ph.D.
Description: First Stillwater River Publications edition. | Pawtucket, RI : Stillwater River Publications, [2019] | Includes bibliographical references.
Identifiers: ISBN 9781950339150 | ISBN 1950339157
Subjects: LCSH: Future life. | Death--Psychological aspects. | Near-death experiences. | Spiritualism.
Classification: LCC BF1311.F8 O47 2019 | DDC 133.9013--dc23

*The views and opinions expressed in this book
are solely those of the author and do not necessarily reflect
the views and opinions of the publisher.*

In memory of my guruji, Yogi Krishan Sidhu,
who started me on this journey.

*Frodo heard a sweet singing running in his mind;
a song that seemed to come like a pale light
behind a grey rain-curtain,
and growing stronger
to turn the veil all to glass and silver,
until at last it was rolled back,
and a far green country opened before him
under a swift sunrise.*
　　　　　　　　　　　　　　　–J.R.R. Tolkien

TABLE OF CONTENTS

Part I

A Note to the Reader .... *i*

Chapter 1 – Is Physical Death the End? 1

Chapter 2 – The Nature of the Afterworld 5

Chapter 3 – Leaving the Body: Reports of the Near-Death Experiencers 11

Chapter 4 – Exceptions: Accidents and Suicides 18

Chapter 5 – The Life Review or the Judgment 23

Chapter 6 – The Resting Place: Soul Slumber 26

Chapter 7 – The Lower Astral Planes: Purgatory, Hell and Earthbound Spirits/Ghosts 29

Chapter 8 – The Middle and Higher Astral Planes 38

Chapter 9 – The Case for Reincarnation 46

Chapter 10 – Returning to an Earth Life 51

Part II

Chapter 1 – Supporting the Dying 59

Chapter 2 – Taking Care of the Dead 63

Chapter 3 – Easing Your Grief 68

Chapter 4 – Supporting the Bereaved 75

Chapter 5 – How Should We Then Live? 78

Appendix
- Yogi Ramacharaka on Spiritual Development 85
- Swami Vishnudevananda on the Sheaths of the Physical Body 87
- Sylvia Browne's "Seven Levels of Advancement in the Afterworld" 89
- Dolores Cannon's Spirit Guide's "Levels of Existence" 91

Favorite Prayers, Affirmations and Quotations 95

Bibliography 103

Recommended Reading 107

A NOTE TO THE READER

All mystics speak the same language, for they come from the same country.
—*Louis Claude de Saint-Martin*

I offer this slim volume because it contains information that I wish I'd had years ago, information I've garnered through many different sources over many decades. I hope this book will not only (Part 1) help readers be less fearful around their own death but also (Part 2) have more tools to support others' passing and their own bereavement process.

Death is universally feared because it is the great Unknown. But it need not be quite so unknown. And though I am not one of them, we now have the reports of the near-death experiencers, mystics, clairvoyants, philosophers, poets, mediums. We have the records of those who, under hypnosis or in trance, have told about the afterworld. We have Plato and the great faith traditions.

My goal is to present the many *commonalities* among all these writings. For this work, I have relied most heavily on the hypnotic regressionist Dolores Cannon, on Yogi Ramacharaka (who my teacher Yogi Krishan assured me is a reliable source) and on the reports of the many near-death experiencers. I hope you will be as amazed as I have been with how closely all these accounts resemble each other and be inspired to read for yourself not only the sources which I have included but also the many others available.

Three beliefs have been held in common throughout time and place. 1) There is a Higher Power, a Supreme Force, an Eternal First Cause. 2) The human spirit does not die with the body—the divine principle within is eternal. And 3) the circumstances of that afterlife depend on the person's character and actions in this life (Ramacharaka 88-9).

Some of this material will be familiar to you and you'll say, "Of course, I know that." Some of this might be as new to you as it once was to me. I'd like to share an example of my process.

I come from a very conservative Christian background, but one day long ago I happened to pick up and read Jess Stearn's book *Yoga, Youth and Reincarnation*. Unlike some of my co-religionists, I did not reject the idea of reincarnation out of hand. Instead, I thought, isn't this *interesting*. After reading other sources, I thought perhaps reincarnation was *possible,* then I went to *probable*. Today, it is part of my *belief* system—but that road was long and carefully traveled.

Plato argued in "Phaedo" that we only know what we, in a sense, *remember*, that is to say, what at a deep level rings true for us, what we 'know in our Knower'—as my Rabbi would say. So I encourage you to accept nothing you read here (no matter what authority asserts it) that does not resonate with you. On the other hand, my hope is that when you meet ideas in this book that are foreign to you, that you, like me, will neither accept them nor reject them, but put them on a mental shelf and notice what other evidence gathers around them—or opposes them.

I'll begin with the comfort afforded us by the reports of the near-death experiencers who subsequently no longer fear death. We can hope for the peace and joy and especially the unconditional love most felt in that state.

But those folks came back. They did not cross the barrier, pass the light at the end of the tunnel or cross the River Styx. This writing not only includes what the near-death experiencers have told us, but also the accounts of those who claim to have seen and spoken to those beyond the barrier while still in the physical—during trance, dream, meditation or hypnotic regression.

The question is,
how far down the rabbit hole do you want to go?
–What the bleep do we know?

PART I

CHAPTER 1

Is Physical Death the End?

I'll look as if I'm dead, and that won't be true. It's too far. I can't take this body with me. It's too heavy. It'll be like an old abandoned shell. There's nothing sad about an old shell.
   –Saint-Exupery, The Little Prince

If you believe that the physical body is all there is, and that when you die you cease to exist, then you agree with Aristotle. But if you think that you are more than your physical body and that when your body dies, you continue to exist, then you side with Plato who asserted the immortality of the soul—that human beings are more than physical and that the non-physical part (which is the real person) never dies. Death is "the release of the soul from the body" (44).

This coincides with the accounts of the near-death experiencers. When they are pronounced dead, they know themselves to be still alive. They report, for example, leaving their body and floating above it, watching the doctors work feverishly on them. When they revive, they can often repeat what was said in the operating room, sometimes to the embarrassment of the medical personnel.

Even though many Jews today have doubts about a life after death, there nevertheless remains in the tradition a belief in an afterlife. A cemetery is called, for example, *Bet Olam* (House of Eternity) or *Bet Ha-Hayyim* (the House of Life). The Kaddish is always said in a worship service, but for the bereaved it is a reminder of the faithfulness of G_d. Jews believe that there is a soul (the sum total of all our deeds and thoughts, habits and character) separate from the body, an immortal soul that lives in the *Olam Haba,* the World to Come. During the funeral, a belief in the afterlife is quoted from Scripture, for example, Isaiah 25.8 "He maketh death to vanish in life eternal; and the Lord G_d wipeth away tears from off all faces..." (Pilkington 99-102).

Christians have always held that there is life after death. Jesus said, "In my Father's house are many mansions... I go to prepare a place for you." John 14:2 St. Paul declared "The things which are seen are temporal; but the things that are not seen are eternal." 2 Cor. 4:18. St. Augustine also believed that the soul, which is immaterial, is the real self and continues after physical death (Parnia 184).

Yoga philosophy, like Plato, teaches that a person is both physical and spiritual; not a body that has a soul, but an "Immortal I" that occupies and uses the body as an instrument. Yoga philosophy delineates even further: that we are in reality several bodies (layers of energy called "sheaths") that cover the soul—each less dense and vibrating at a higher frequency than the preceding. Like light waves or radio waves, our body's sheaths interpenetrate but do not interfere with each other. (For additional information, see Vishnudevanda 12-20 and Van Praagh 28-32 in the Appendix.)

Tibetan Buddhism is similar to the Yoga tradition in that it postulates three bodies: the gross (the physical), the subtle (an energy body) and the extremely subtle body, "the deepest level of which is the level of pure awareness, which Tibetans call the mind of clear light" (Berkson 109). My guess is that this last refers to union with God.

Moslems believe in a life after death—that all beings are created by God and all return to God (in an *embodied* state, however). But not immediately. Except for martyrs who go directly to Paradise, the dead lie in the grave between death and the resurrection (Berkson 84-5).

It is common knowledge that the Egyptians believed in a life after physical death (especially for the pharaoh), a life like this one, only better. Pyramid texts are about awakening, experiencing judgment, ascending through the sky to the next world and being admitted into the company of the gods. The Egyptians practiced mummification because without a body, it was harder for them to imagine life.

Like the Yogis, our physicists tell us that all matter is, in reality, energy; that energy is all that exists—including our physical bodies. Energy can change form, but is neither created nor destroyed. If we believe the physicists, then Plato, not Aristotle was right—and we live on.

The body is mortal, but the person dwelling in the body is immortal and immeasurable.
   –Bhagavad Gita

CHAPTER 2

The Nature of the Afterworld*

Energy is all there is,
and it fills up the all that there is.
It's all energy.
—A person in trance to Dolores Cannon

As mentioned in the previous chapter, our physicists tell us that all matter is, in reality, energy—and energy is all that exists. Energy can change form, but is neither created nor destroyed. The afterworld (the non-physical reality) is energy and, according to many reports, can be accessed while we are still in the physical. The veil is much thinner than we ordinarily imagine. Think of those with paranormal abilities, abilities that they say we all have but few of us can access.

---

*Also known as the Astral World or the Invisible World.

you've read reports of people who sense when a distant loved one is in trouble, for example. Some can tell who is calling them on the phone before they answer; others report seeing ghosts and feeling presences.

The afterworld cannot be a physical existence though some traditions speaking of resurrection seem to indicate that. For example, could Jesus have been resurrected in a *physical* body, walk through walls and appear and disappear at will? The New Testament tells that Jesus appeared to men on the road to Emmaus who spoke with him, but did not recognize him until the meal and the breaking of the bread. And then he disappeared. After his death, he was not only able to manifest (like the ghosts we read about) but, if we believe the accounts, was also able to manifest solidly enough that he could share fish with the disciples by the Galilee.

Because we living persons inhabit the physical world, we tend to think of the afterworld in physical and spatial terms. Heaven is up, hell is down. But the afterworld is not an objective *place* in space. It is not material, of course; it is an *energy state* or condition, a vibratory energy frequency which is all around us (Ramacharaka 26).

John O'Donohue paraphrases Meister Eckart: "the eternal world does not seem to be a place but rather a different state of being… the dead are here with us, in the air that we are moving through all the time" (226). Deborah King writes the same when she says that it was "Mary Baker Eddy's belief that after you die, you don't really go anywhere. She felt that the next plane was a continuation of whatever you had created while here on Earth…." (133). Psychic Sylvia Browne discovered in her NDE that "The Other Side isn't some distant paradise beyond the clouds. It really exists right here among us, only three feet above our ground level simply in another dimension with a much higher vibration than ours" (49).

The near-death experiencers, those in hypnotic trance, mediums and the yogis say further that this non-physical reality is composed of many "planes" and "sub-planes" (Ramacharaka 35) which differ in their rate of vibration—but no *physical* higher up or lower down. However, for the sake of ease of understanding, I'll speak of lower or higher planes. By "lower" planes, I mean those more dense, more material, of a *slower* vibration. By "higher" planes I mean those that are less dense, more spiritual, of a *higher* vibration.

Like the sheaths of our physical bodies and like radio waves, telephone messages and light waves, these "planes" exist together but do not interfere with each other.

Those who tell us of these planes, say that a person's plane in the afterlife is determined, *not by her religious beliefs, but by her spiritual development reflected in her vibrational frequency.* A person "will gravitate to the particular level of the astral world that corresponds to the frequency of its astral body's vibration" (Van Praagh 48). She goes to the plane for which she is most suited, where she feels most at home, where she will be the happiest (Ramacharaka 63). If her focus in life was on the material/earthly/physical, she arrives at a lower vibrational plane; the more spiritual her focus and desires, the vibrationally higher the plane.

The writers assert that when a person dies, he finds himself where he expects to be. Think of the Native Americans' "happy hunting ground" or the Christians' "City of Gold." Now, if a person thinks he deserves the lake of fire because of the way he's lived his life, that's exactly what he'll see. According to Ramacharaka (101-02), when he realizes that he's created that scenario, he can create a different reality. If, however, he believes he'll go to paradise, that's where he'll think he is. Remember that the afterworld is energy, not material.

Of all the writers, Ramacharaka alone reassures us that each soul will find the religious environment he adopted in his earthly life: not only the heaven or hell he believed in, but the persons of similar faith as well as the prophets and founders of his religion (93-4).

> In the afterworld "thoughts become things." And each plane is the result of the composite mental images of those inhabiting that particular plane. Again, we get what we expect, what we project. Which is not to say that there aren't "real" constructions that are experienced by many people (Ramacharaka 82).

The inhabitants of the afterworld, writers say, all appear around thirty years old and in perfect health no matter their age or physical condition when they died. Persons can appear in whatever clothing suits them at the time and still be recognized. Conversation is transmitted by thought, not words. There is, of course, no marriage or sex as the afterworld is an energy state not a physical/material one. (In Matt. 22:30 Jesus is quoted as saying, "In the resurrection they neither marry, nor are given in marriage, but are as the angels of God in heaven.")

Can we see each other and visit anyone we wish on other planes? Well, apparently not. A person on a lower plane cannot go visiting on a higher. A person on a higher plane can, however, visit someone on a lower if that person wishes comfort or companionship or spiritual help. It's not that the person inhabiting the lower plane is refused entrance to the higher—his vibration is too dense. A crude analogy is stones in a sieve: the finer stones can go through to where the larger are—but not the reverse. Advanced souls can minister to those on a lower plane (Ramacharaka 75). I am reminded of the story of the rich man and Lazarus. Lazarus could, theoretically, visit the rich man, but not the reverse.

I'm guessing that my readers' interest is now inclined toward the reports of the near-death experiencers. Note that discussion of the planes and sub-planes in the Astral or Afterworld continues in chapters 7 and 8 on the Lower, Middle and Higher Planes.

CHAPTER 3

Leaving the Body: Reports of the Near-Death Experiencers

Death is a release—like an escape from prison.
–Starr Wright

Death is a *process* in which the astral body separates from the physical body. (Note that according to the yogis, the astral body is not the soul, but one of the coverings or sheaths of the soul.) This process can take a while, and in the case of near-death experiencers (NDEs), is reversed, of course. They come back into the physical—and we have their stories.

The elements of that process have been fully outlined by Raymond Moody in his *Paranormal* (86-9), though he states that not all experiencers include all these elements. I think Moody's list is a great starting point; I will elaborate on some of the elements.

1. If the person dies in a hospital, he usually hears the doctor pronounce him dead. Physical senses diminish, psychical senses increase. (Note that hearing is the last <u>physical</u> sense to go—so it's important to be very careful what one says around the dying.) Some experiencers hear a buzzing sound.

2. There is often a sense of exhilaration so the person wonders why these people are crying. The dying person usually feels that he's drifting upward toward the ceiling and can look down and see himself on the operating table, but he feels no pain. Sometimes the person in his astral body leaves the room or even the hospital—or the continent!

3. The individual becomes aware of incredible—but not hurtful *light*—and feels great *peace, calm*—and especially *love*. There is no more pain. The experience is so wonderful that the dying person often does not want to return when, in the case of an NDE, he is given a choice and does indeed return.

4. He is not left alone. Greeters or astral helpers meet him—often he recognizes people he has known in this life or in another. The communication is mental, a rapport versus words/sounds. People he has known who have passed on appear in healthy middle age. If the person has a deep belief in a spiritual being, that spirit's energy will be there for him.

5. Most report a Being of Light and Love which they identify according to their religious belief.

6. The person then has a Life Review (a Judgment, if you will) and sees in a flash all the experiences of his life, even the most seemingly inconsequential.

7. Ultimately, he comes to a border, a limit: it can be a bright light at the end of a tunnel, a river, a mist, a door, a fence, a line. Since these are the reports of experiencers, they do not cross that barrier, but choose instead to return to their physical (often painful) body. (Note that the astral body is attached to the physical body by a 'silver cord'; once that energy cord is broken, there is no re-entering the body.)

What Shall Come Hereafter

8. Upon return, he tries to tell others about his experience and is usually not believed. He then often becomes reserved and stops telling his story.

9. The experience, however, normally has a profound effect; these people have new goals, heightened moral principles and strive to live with love, kindness and compassion. And they no longer fear death.

The first recorded experience of an NDE is in Plato's Republic (as quoted in Sam Parnia's *Erasing Death*).

> An ordinary soldier suffers a near-fatal injury on the battlefield and is revived in the funeral parlor. He describes a journey from darkness to light, accompanied by guides, a moment of judgment, feelings of peace and joy, and visions of extraordinary beauty and happiness. (150).

In *Jesus and the Essenes* when Dolores Cannon asked Katherine during a past life regression as "Suddi" about what happens at death, he said:

> There are many things in our writings, yes. It speaks of the feeling of great peace that descends upon one. When you look down upon yourself and realize that you have passed over the threshold. That you are no longer one with the physical and are a being that is totally what you would call a soul again, or a spirit. There are people who are confused (after they die). They would be greeted by someone who would perhaps help smooth the pathways that they must walk. And all who are there to help, wish you well. There is no need to fear, for nothing can harm you. (117)

Cannon (and many other authors) notes that the process of dying is *the same irrespective of religious belief.* All religions (speaking of death) focus on peace, serenity and judgment/retribution. And *light.* Ps. 104: 1-2 "O Lord my God... who coverest thyself with light as with a garment," I John 1:5 "God is light." (Isn't it interesting that Dante does not describe God except as *Light*?)

The Being of Light is variously identified according to the person's religious beliefs. Since he was a Christian, George Ritchie in his book *Return from Tomorrow* identified this Light as a person, specifically as the Son of God—as, by the way, did Howard Storm in *My Descent into Death*. They both felt profoundly and unconditionally loved—which is the consistent report of the NDEs.

Unfortunately, not all NDEs initially have a pleasant time. Storm at first had a far different experience. He said he was an atheist and had lived a life "devoted to building a monument to my ego. My family, my sculptures, my painting, my house, my gardens, my little fame, my illusions of power, were all an extension of my ego" (21). When he left his body, he found himself excruciatingly tormented in hell—until he cried out to Jesus to save him. And then a light which he identified as Jesus came toward him and took him out of hell. As a side note, I found his story at first horrifying and then profoundly instructive and inspiring.

These near-death experiencers allay one of our deepest fears. Yes, even after physical death, we are still the person we know ourselves to be. You are still you. Your personality remains intact. One moment you have a physical existence, the next you are in a non-physical reality—but you still have your memories. You feel like your life is still continuing—which, according to their accounts, it is.

CHAPTER 4

Exceptions: Accidents and Suicides

They cannot realize that they have passed out of the body and are often sorely perplexed.
            —Yogi Ramacharaka

Sudden unexpected deaths—murder, suicide and accident victims—including those persons in hospitals not expecting to die, are exceptions to the happy NDE pattern in that they do not, of course, come back to life. The real problem is that *the dead person may be very confused and not know he is dead.* He may look at his body in the bed (or on the pavement), for example, and wonder what's happened, why folks ignore him and act as if they neither hear nor see him, as if he no longer exists. He is confused and needs the help that is there for him.

Note that people experiencing unexpected death are not left alone. Astral helpers or departed friends or family members will come to them and explain the situation and help them cross over when they're willing to do so. We, the living, can also help by praying for them and talking to them.

Even during times of huge calamities like massive earthquakes, train or airplane wrecks or battles when many die at once, Ramacharaka sets our mind at ease by telling us there are reports of advanced persons still in the physical who leave in their astral body to help minister to these persons (55).

From all I've read, suicides have a more difficult time. They may remember taking their life but, thinking that death is the end, like those not expecting death, they also are confused and don't know where they are. We can help. As a personal example, after my stepson took his life, an extraordinary friend of mine helped him by going into an altered state, located him drifting around in the dark and told him to look up and go to the light. She reported that he did so. I can't verify what happened, of course, except that I felt profound relief.

When Parnia (*Erasing Death)*, began his study of NDEs, he noted their consistent positive experiences regardless of religious or cultural background. The exceptions, unfortunately, were those who had attempted suicide. "In those cases, people who survived described some very unpleasant traumatic and painful experiences that did not match those who had died involuntarily or from natural causes" (138). (Also note Sylvia Browne pp. 65-6.)

Suicide has never been condoned, never been universally viewed as a viable option. Life is sacred. We have been given the gift of life and it is not our prerogative to take that life. Suicide is casting off the body prematurely; it is breaking the life contract, giving up on a problem instead of working it out (Cannon 128).* Hamlet would have committed suicide if "the Everlasting had not fixed his canon 'gainst self-slaughter." Again, the narrator in Plato's "Phaedo" said that Socrates is "willing to die—though he will not take his own life for that is held not to be right" (38).

Sadly, suicide doesn't solve anything. A person in a past-life regression was told that the suicide victim in another or next life must face and overcome an equally great challenge.

---

* *For reading ease, all references to Dolores Cannon are from her* Between Death and Life *unless otherwise specified.*

"The killing of self is the ultimate wrong because that throws the karma out of balance" (Cannon 129). And creates more karma. In *Jesus and the Essenes*, the person regressed to the time of Christ said, surprisingly enough, that Judas' worse sin was not his betrayal, but his suicide (246).

The good news: you can help.

To allay the confusion of the accident or suicide victim, talk to them—*tell them what's happened and that they are dead*; they have passed out of their physical body, but they are not alone. *Tell them to ask for help, to look up and see the light and the divine helpers—and go toward them.*

Tell the suicide victim to let go of guilt, that he is forgiven; he did the best he could under the circumstances. He will get another chance at an earthly life and this time, hopefully, he will not give up.

Pray for the suicide or sudden death victim. Read their sacred scriptures. Reassure them that they are very much missed. Send them thoughts of love and peace.

I like the Tibetan Buddhist advice for helping someone who has died a sudden or violent death:

What Shall Come Hereafter

Imagine tremendous rays of light emanating from the buddhas or divine beings, pouring down all their compassion and blessing. Imagine this light streaming down onto the dead person, purifying them totally and freeing them from the confusion and pain of their death, granting them profound, lasting peace. (Rinpoche 302)

See also: **Chapter 13: Easing Your Grief**

CHAPTER 5

The Life Review or the Judgment

A human being fashions his consequences as surely as he fashions his goods or his dwelling. Nothing that he says, thinks or does is without consequences.

–Norman Cousins

Everything that I have read indicates that after leaving the body, the person has a Life Review; the Bible refers to this as the Last Judgment—often anticipated with dread even by devout Christians.

Like the other near death experiencers, George Ritchie had his life review. He saw in a moment of time (in the presence of a brilliant light which he identified as Jesus) the panorama of his entire life: consequential and inconsequential events. He not only saw all the actions of his life, but felt the results of those actions—he felt the hurt he had caused others. The important point is that the Light did not judge him; his own conscience was the judge. I quote Ritchie.

> It was I who was judging the events around us so harshly. It was I who saw them as trivial, self-centered, unimportant. No such condemnation came from the Glory shining around me. He was not blaming or reproaching. He was simply… loving me… waiting for my answer to the question that still hung in the dazzling air. "What have you done with your life to show Me?" The question, like everything else proceeding from Him, had to do with love. How much have you loved with your life? Have you loved others as I am loving you? (54)

Dr. Sam Parnia asserted the same thing, that the Life Review is a *self-judgment* during which the person feels the pain and distress he's caused others (130).

In one of Dolores Cannon's past life regression conversations, she remarked to the subject, "I have been told there is no punishment no matter what we do." The spirit responded, "There most certainly is punishment. And the worse punishment of all is that punishment which we deal ourselves. *We are our own judge and jury*" (113-14).

Yogi Ramacharaka states more than once "Each man is his own absolute law-giver, the dispenser of glory or gloom to himself, the decreer of his own life, his reward, his punishment" (106). If a person's own conscience is the judge, it follows that he judges himself "according to the highest standards of his own soul, which, of course, represent the standards of his time and environment" (98). He passes judgment on all below his standard; it is actual justice, without hypocrisy or self-deception. In the Yogi's analogy, we don't condemn the fox for stealing a chicken—that's his nature. A lower spiritually developed soul has a less developed sense of right and wrong—and judges himself accordingly.

This assertion that the judgment after death is a self-judgment comes to me as both a relief and a warning to monitor my life now, a reminder to strive to live in kindness, love, service, forgiveness—and self-forgiveness. We are all doing the best we can given the circumstances and our spiritual development at the time.

CHAPTER 6

The Resting Place: Soul-Slumber

As an eagle, weary after soaring in the sky, folds its wings and flies down to rest in its nest, so does the shining Self enter the state of dreamless sleep, where one is freed from all desires.

–Brihadaranyaka Upanishad

After a person has left his physical life and has had his Life Review, he often goes to the Resting Place and sleeps in preparation for his awakening in the spiritual world. This is a place of forgetfulness and healing especially if his last life was very traumatic—accident victims, suicides and victims of the Holocaust, for example (Cannon 50). What we are calling the 'resting place' is, of course, not a *place* but a state or condition, a condition in which the person in soul-slumber is absolutely protected, calm, safe, secure and guarded. No harm can come to him.

Yogi Ramacharaka tells us that soul-slumber is like being in a coma or like the state of the human unborn child in the womb preparing to awaken on the earth plane. After its soul slumber, the soul sheds its astral shell and is being prepared for its rebirth on the spiritual plane. Think of the butterfly in the chrysalis that has 'died' to his caterpillar life only to emerge in a new and glorious state (48).

I love it that Browne calls this state "Co-cooning" in which "the spirit is put into a restful, healing twilight sleep and receives constant care and a steady infusion of God's compassion, peace and kind empowering love" (83).

Normally the person in soul-slumber is indeed totally calm and at peace. But those 1) who have unfinished earth business or 2) have died consumed by addictions, anger, revenge, regret or 3) are suicides or 4) are being called back to earth by the cries of the bereaved are restless and resist soul-slumber—sometimes for years. They have not dropped their astral shell and they try to return to earth. They are sometimes seen as ghosts in their old haunts or around graves (Ramacharaka 48-54).

What Shall Come Hereafter

The time in soul-slumber varies depending on the person's spiritual development: the greater his development, the more sheaths he can drop off and the longer his sleep.

Whether the time is short or long, he eventually awakens on the plane which corresponds to the highest and best in him according to his level of spiritual development. It is the plane for which he is most suited, where he is the happiest and has the most opportunity to progress. He is with others who share his interests and with whom he can have the best companionship. It's that person's version of heaven—and there he can fulfill aspirations and gain wisdom (Ramacharaka 61-4).

Opinions differ, of course. Moslems as well as Martin Luther and St. Augustine believed that the dead sleep until the resurrection (Berkson 77). John Calvin, on the other hand, believed that there was no sleep; people went immediately to Heaven or Hell and waited for their resurrection in a physical body (79).

CHAPTER 7

The Lower Astral Planes: Purgatory, Hell and Earthbound Spirits/Ghosts

If you want to know what happens after you die, watch the movie "Ghosts."
—Yogi Krishan Sidhu

The Lower planes and sub-planes can be thought of as part of the earth, a sort of blending of the earth plane and the astral or spiritual planes. These vibratory levels (they are not physical, of course) are there all the time. The veil between these lower planes and the earth is thin; some people can see their inhabitants as ghosts, but these spirits are invisible to most of us. Some disembodied spirits have the power to materialize in order to bring us messages or comfort.

Think of the reports of Jesus appearing to followers after his death.

Purgatory is found in Catholic theology, but not in Protestantism. Like the Buddhist *bardo*, it is sort of a holding place in preparation for Heaven. Ramacharaka identifies it as one of the sub-planes of the Lower Astral (39). Browne's The Holding Place is "an anteroom before the Godless darkness behind The Left Door... the residents are spirits who spend their lives on this earth in that vast gray area between The Dark Side and the divine light of God" (64). All belief systems assert that our prayers encouraging the person to call upon God can shorten their time there.

The Bible, the Qur'an, the Yogis, the NDEs, the mediums, the psychics, Dante, Milton and even Plato all speak of a Hell. The most common imagery is darkness, burning flames and never ending torment. Van Praagh notes that this plane vibrates at a much slower rate, the light is dim, and "a pungent and unpleasant odor pervades it." Spirits here harbor "hate, malice, and the need for control over others.... They can be murderers, rapists, thieves, swindlers, cheaters, assassins, or anyone who has harmed another human being" (61).

Browne has a different take which I've not read any place else. She describes hell not particularly as an astral plane, but as behind The Left Door taken by the dying who, in their earth life rejected God and his love, "true sociopaths, remorseless and amoral," and "criminals that can't be rehabilitated—without social conscience" (61-2). When such a person dies, she says, he never experiences the tunnel or the sacred light, but goes through that door into "an abyss of dark, Godless, empty, joyless, all-encompassing nothingness." (Sounds like Milton's *Paradise Lost*.) Browne writes that these spirits "travel straight from their bodies at death, through the Godless darkness they've chosen, and right back in utero again…that leaves them as dark at birth as they were at death in their previous life" (63).

Some theologians have questioned whether the language of Hell (and Heaven) is literal or metaphorical. In 1999, Pope John II described Heaven and Hell as states of the soul rather than literal places, that is, Heaven is a state in communion with God, Hell is alienation from God (Berkson 78). Protestants usually hold that both are *places*, which goes along with their literal scriptural interpretation. Some belief systems propose that hell is eternal; others that it is a temporary state.

I personally never thought of hell as a real (though immaterial) place until I read Howard Storm's NDE experience reported in his *My Descent into Death*. And Rajiv Parti's NDE account in *Dying to Wake Up*. Dr. Parti found himself at the rim of hell, heard the anguished cries of sufferers, felt the heat, smelled smoke and burning flesh. He heard a voice say, "You have clearly not been making love." And "You have led a materialistic and selfish life" (29-30). This was an NDE, so of course he came back into his physical body—and, as most NDE experiencers, radically changed his life.

Ghosts are the astral forms of *disembodied spirits* living in the lower planes because they are still attracted to earth; many recently died and have not completed their transition to spiritual planes. They often attend their own funeral and haunt their grave. These disembodied spirits are visible to those with psychic ability and those having an NDE. Interestingly enough, ghosts can also be the astral bodies of *living people* who can travel to these planes during sleep, trance conditions or astral projection.

D'Anne Olsen

When George Ritchie had his NDE, Jesus showed him a vast plane on which disembodied spirits fought in vain to kill each other (63-7). He was also taken inside a bar where he noted that the actual drinkers had an electrical field around them (the aura)—but other folks did not. Eventually he realized that those others were dead but not realizing their state, they nevertheless kept trying to grab a glass and get a drink but, being in spirit form, could not. The most appalling part of his account for me was his report of watching the protective aura of a drunken (unconscious) man split open from the crown—and a ghost pop in and disappear (59-61).

Ritchie was also shown scenes of ghosts frustrated because they were not seen or heard by the living that they so desperately wanted to communicate with. Particularly poignant for me were the suicides crying out to their grieving and unhearing loved ones over and over how sorry they were (58-9). But of course they could only be seen or heard by those with psychic ability. A friend of mine recounted this very experience: a psychic saw my friend's nephew who had committed suicide calling out to his mother begging forgiveness.

What Shall Come Hereafter

Dolores Cannon notes these categories of earthbound spirits:

1. Some ghosts appear as sleepwalkers, not aware of their surroundings. They are trapped in a moment of time and act out the same scene over and over. Out of fear, they hang on to a mental construct because their subconscious hasn't yet figured out they're dead. These spirits are in transition—they haven't crossed over and don't see their astral helpers. Poltergeists, on the other hand, are aware of their surroundings and have the ability to move objects. They seek attention—sometimes revenge. They can haunt houses and play tricks on those who live there (173).

2. Other spirits, filled with remorse, don't go to their proper place in the astral world. Instead, they wander about on the earth plane keeping to their old haunts trying in vain to complete unfinished business or to make up for misdeeds. A few are "so attached personally to souls left behind in the flesh, that they brood over the loved persons, impotently striving to aid and guide them" (Ramacharka 148). Others are held earth-bound by the over-grieving of loved ones calling them back (Cannon172-3).

3. Some spirits appear in séances, sometimes impersonating loved ones or historical figures (Ramacharaka 148). These spirits tend to reincarnate very quickly because they want to be back on earth. Most sources deeply discourage trying to communicate with the dead. I'm reminded of King Saul's asking the Witch of Endor (1 Sam. 28) to call up the spirit of Samuel. It didn't turn out well.

Raymond Moody researched what the Greeks called "oracles of the dead". He created the "Reunions Experiment" (195) for grieving clients in Alabama in which clients could spend the day in a sort of cave with mirrors and call up their dead relative and hold a conversation. He had 80% success rate which means it is possible, but is it fair to those who have passed on? Shouldn't we rather send them love and wishes for their spiritual progress instead of "drag them back to the lower plane of materiality to hear them say that they are happy and that all is all right with them?" (Ramacharaka 141)

Can we help these ghosts/disembodied spirits? Yes.

We can pray for them and send them to the light in the name of Christ. We can ask their guardian angels to help them find the plane where they will be happiest. If we realize we are holding the dead earthbound with our excessive grief, we can tell our loved ones that we are okay and that they need to leave us and continue with their progress in the spiritual world.

Can we protect ourselves and our homes from malignant or annoying earthbound spirits? Yes.

Ramacharaka tells us that if we give an authoritative command to leave, they must do so. Cannon is more specific. We can tell the ghost, "'I bid you leave in the name of Christ,' and it must go. It has to obey this name, they have no choice" (Cannon 162). Dowsers tell us to send them to the light where they can be healed. When the terrified Hamlet saw the ghost of his father, he called out for supernatural help: "Angels and ministers of grace defend us!" My own favorite protection protocol comes from Cannon as well as from dowser friend Tom Milliren. Visualizing myself in a pyramid or egg of light, I say *"I cover myself with the white light of Christ. Only good can come to me, only good can come from me."* I've used this not only for self-protection upon occasion, but also to protect my car and even my house.

CHAPTER 8

Middle and Higher Astral Planes

What happens after death is so unspeakably glorious that our imagination and feelings do not suffice to form even an approximate conception of it.
  –Carl Jung

Just as all spiritual traditions speak of a Hell, they all also speak of a Heaven, but differ on who will go there. Some Christians believe that only the "saved" are admitted. Others, including C.S. Lewis, postulate that even non-Christians could get into Heaven, but by the power of Jesus—whether or not they knew him by that name. In other words, those who follow the best and highest of their own religion will be included—read Lewis' *The Last Battle*. The Hindu Vedas say that "the Supreme One accepts all (such) worship when honestly given as intended for itself" (Ramacharaka 91).

What many call "Heaven," a spirit guide (reported by Cannon) called "Paradise". It can be thought of as a middle astral plane or a higher *earth* plane, a perfected earth where many people go when they die; it's a transitional plane. There are hills, mountains, valleys. All is more beautiful, the colors of flowers more vibrant than we ever experience here. Ramacharaka calls it "a plane of Nature which is fuller, richer, sweeter in every way than the best of which the earth-dwelling soul dreams" (133). The inhabitants can manifest houses with their favorite furniture, boats, resorts and so on. If the person wants to, he can go fishing or gardening or visit family and friends.

This apparently is the most popular plane where folks are waiting for their next earth life (Cannon 36-7). And this may be what Jesus was referring to when he said, "In my father's house are many mansions." This "paradise" seems to me to be what the Egyptians described—similar to earth but so much better. And the plane that Plato was referring to when he said that the earth is a reflection of the spiritual world—and not the other way around. The spiritual world, in other words, is the *real* world. C.S. Lewis (*The Great Divorce*) was getting at the same idea when he described heaven as more *solid* than earth.

If the mid-astral is beautiful, the higher planes are absolutely glorious. These, Cannon writes, are inhabited by the most spiritually developed souls who on these planes experience bliss unimaginable. They continue to grow in wisdom and can serve on the general councils or, during alternate astral lifetimes, serve as guides, teachers and helpers to specific people both on the astral planes and on the earth. They can stay for centuries in these higher planes or reincarnate 1) in order to manifest the growth achieved or 2) when they feel the desire for new experience or 3) if they wish to join friends and loved ones on earth.

Although I found that the reports of those who traveled in NDE (Ritchie), trance or hypnosis to the middle and higher planes differ somewhat in where buildings are located, the accounts give us a consistent general description.

On all the planes there are schools where the Masters are perceived as ectoplasms in white robes teaching in magnificent white pillared rooms. There are rooms where you can learn, grow, and satisfy various aspirations—in the sciences, philosophy, music or art, for example. You can develop talents and genius that can manifest in your next incarnation (Cannon 37-8).

Unlike most NDE accounts that I've read, George Ritchie *(Return from Tomorrow)* reported visiting these planes. He saw a study center "humming with the excitement of great discovery," (69) "a studio where music of a complexity I couldn't begin to follow was being composed and performed." He walked through the Library where he thought were "all the works of the universe" (70). He went into a building with technological machinery and saw a sphere-shaped structure. Nine years later he saw illustrated in a 1952 Life magazine "a *drawing of the prototype of the second US atomic submarine engine"* which he recognized from his NDE (120).

Dolores Cannon recorded a person in a hypnotic state who visited classrooms in what she called the School of Knowledge. This person saw the Akashic Records, the Book of Life in which each person can find what they are looking for since all that one has experienced is written there. She was assured that there is no danger for a living person in trance to look at their records because the subconscious does not allow access to anything that is detrimental to the living person. This person in trance, however, was told that it is not good to delve much into one's personal future (36).

Cannon's spirit guide tells us that in the Upper Astral there is a "beautiful jewel-like city". We've read of this city not only in Cannon's *Between Death and Life*, but also in the "Revelation of St. John," in Milton's *Paradise Lost*, and in Ritchie's *Return from Tomorrow* to name just a few sources. I quote Ritchie's description of the city.

> A glowing, seemingly endless city, bright enough to be seen over the unimaginable distance between. The brightness seemed to shine from the very walls and streets of this place, and from beings which I could now discern moving about within it. In fact, the city and everything in it seemed to be made of light, even as this figure (Jesus) at my side was made of light. (72)

The City, says Cannon, contains the **Temple of Wisdom Complex** which houses the Temple of Healing, the Tapestry Room and the Library (62).

The **Temple of Healing** is a Chamber of Color and Light, a beautiful rotunda with multicolored glass windows. Cannon's person in hypnotic trance described it "like being inside a jewel box." Amazingly, a person (as in this account) can go there while still in the physical body—and experience the healing of his astral body which healed his physical body on earth. He also noted that if a person died from a long-term illness or severe accident, he can go there instead of to the resting place to be healed (67).

The **Library,** which Ritchie visited and which Browne calls the Hall of Records**,** houses books, scrolls and manuscripts on *everything*. There is a scriptorium for medium advanced souls who like to read. And a viewing room, akin to a computer room, for more advanced souls (Cannon 76). In the astral library, information can be accessed so the person returns to the earth plane with increased "intuition." For example, inventors, philosophers and scientists can manifest on earth the knowledge they have acquired on the astral planes.

Like the Library, th**e Tapestry Room** can be accessed during meditation, hypnotic trance or astral projection (Cannon 68). This room houses a very, very tall tapestry (20-25 feet high). It is interwoven with metal threads that sparkle—"like a living thing". Each thread represents a life; some are tiny strings, some are rope size. It is a visual illustration of the oneness of all humanity. The observer reported that the tapestry "goes into the higher dimensions, even above here....everything ends in Godhood where it's all brightness" (71).

Another spirit between lives spoke of being in a **General Council** which Browne says is housed in the Hall of Justice which is surrounded by "endless, achingly beautiful Gardens" (105). The general council, reports Cannon, is held in an oval lecture hall seeming to hang in air but which was actually supported by a deep violet energy field. The room was enclosed by golden pillars, was encircled by tiers on which sat spirits appearing as bright balls of light. A magnificent gold podium stood in the center. The work of the general council was to see the overall pattern of (energy) events and try to maximize positive energy effects and minimize negative ones (197).

At the conclusion of Cannon's chapter on "The General Council," she adds this paragraph—and I quote in full.

> I have been told that in addition to the general councils, there are also numerous levels of councils above them. I don't know if there is any limit, as I have been told of

universal councils that are over entire universes and also councils on the Creator level. The ones on that level are considered co-creators with God and work on creating new universes or whatever is needed, *ad infinitum*. (203)

Those on the highest planes of the upper astral (next to the Divine Energy or the Godhead), Cannon notes, learn to be a universal spirit and don't usually incarnate except for a particular mission. A spirit told her, "Great men in history, for instance, Jesus and Buddha have been very high upper-astral entities that did come back" (84).

For further delineation of the planes, refer to Browne's and Cannon's "Levels" in the Appendix.

Note: I think no one puts the contrast between the lower and upper Astral Planes better than Ritchie. In his NDE, he contrasts the beings he saw in the lower hellish realm "trapped in some form of *self-attention*" with those in schools in the higher planes: "they appeared utterly and supremely *self-forgetful*—absorbed in some vast purpose beyond themselves" (68-69). Italics mine. I first met this contrast in C.S. Lewis' writings.

CHAPTER 9

The Case for Reincarnation

Never was there a time when I did not exist, nor you, nor in the future shall any of us cease to be. For the soul there is neither birth or death, nor having once been does it cease to be.

–Bhagavad Gita

Not only do the Buddhist and Hindu traditions espouse reincarnation, but "Early Christianity also embraced reincarnation until Pope Anastasias condemned it as blasphemy in A.D. 400, and the 'monstrous doctrine' of reincarnation was declared anathema at the Second Council of Constantinople in 553" (King 140). Those early Christian theologians who embraced reincarnation include St. Augustine, Clement of Alexandria, St. Gregory of Nyssa, Justin Martyr,

Origen of Alexandria, St. Jerome and the Gnostics.

A few New Testament gospel passages seem to indicate belief in reincarnation. For example, some folks thought that John the Baptist was Elijah come again. In John 9:2, Jesus is asked if this man or his parents sinned that he was *born* blind, i.e. that he sinned in a previous lifetime. When Jesus asked his disciples who people said he is, they answered, "Some say that thou art John the Baptist; some Elias; and others, Jeremias, or one of the prophets" (Matt. 16:14). Also, Jesus says "…Elias is come already and they knew him not….Then the disciples understood that he spake unto them of John the Baptist" (Matt. 17: 12,3).

Brian Weiss notes that in Judaism there was a belief in reincarnation until about 1800-1850. He quotes Rabbi Moshe Chaim Luzzatto in *The Way of God.* "A single soul can be reincarnated a number of times in different bodies, and in this manner, it can rectify the damage done in previous incarnations. Similarly, it can also attain perfection that was not attained in its previous incarnation" (40**).**

In *The Thirteen Petalled Rose*, a book by Adin Steinsaltz commenting on the Jewish Kabala, we read, "After the death of the body, the soul is reincarnated in the body of another person and again must try and complete what it failed to correct or what it injured in the past" (64).

During Dr Parti's NDE, his father told him that his many past lives were connected to this present. "You now know that your challenges from the past are presented to you again...You have another life and another chance to cure your addictions" (34). This conversation occurring in his NDE illustrates the purpose of reincarnation: to attain perfection.

Pythagoras and Plato believed in reincarnation. In his "Phaedo", Plato wrote "I am confident in the belief that there truly is such a thing as living again, and that the living spring from the dead, and that the souls of the dead are in existence, and that the good souls have a better portion than the evil" (49).

Moody had a past-life regression session in which he experienced nine past lives. These and many, many other accounts of (often verified) past lives don't *prove* reincarnation of course, but they suggest its credibility.

Do we incarnate into physical form endlessly? Most traditions say not. Yogi Ramacharaka writes that the purpose of reincarnation is spiritual growth so that eventually one joins the Divine. He asserts that the series of physical reincarnations is not endless. As in Plato, the material universe is illusory—the spiritual world is the real world. Not the body but the *soul* will persist even after earth has its end. It will continue realm after realm, rising higher and higher until it reaches liberation (182).

Hinduism teaches the cycle (Samsara) of birth-suffering-death-rebirth. The goal is liberation from the cycle. In the *Upanishads* we learn that rebirths are controlled by Karma, so if we stop making Karma, we stop rebirth and achieve liberation—to be forever in the presence of Brahman, the Ultimate Reality (Berkson 93).

In Buddhism as well, the cycle of death and rebirth is driven by Karma and the goal is, again, to get off the cycle. The realms of rebirth are temporary, seen by some as places, some as psychological or metaphorical states (Berkson 103-4).

If we choose to affirm the validity of reincarnation, it follows that we have experienced reincarnation many times. For me, though, the best advice around past lives is from my teacher, Yogi Krishan: "Don't concern yourself with your past lives. This life is the most important," and I might add, it is most important to live this life in such a way that we make the best preparation for the afterworld—and any possible future incarnations.

CHAPTER 10

Returning to an Earth Life

Being born in the physical world provides the greatest opportunities for spiritual growth and realization, and choosing a good incarnation requires discrimination and some conscious awareness.

–Deborah King

One does not *have to* return to a physical life, but since more progress can be made on the earth plane than in the astral, after a certain amount of time, one usually chooses to reincarnate. You'll recall that it's all about spiritual development—reaching perfection, becoming one with the Godhead. To that end, living a physical life is more efficient—though certainly more challenging—than continuing in the astral.

When the time comes that a person in the astral world wishes to return to another life in the physical, she goes through planning sessions with the masters and teachers assigned to help her make her contract. She decides what lessons she wants to learn, what karma she needs to balance, what tasks she wants to accomplish, what abilities she's acquired in the astral that she wants to manifest. If her most recent earth life has been very difficult, she might choose a *resting life* in which she just seems to drift along without much challenge (Cannon 51-2).

In this preparatory time, she also consults with the other people that she intends to work out karmic issues with—or whose lives she wants to share. Of course, she may have to wait until the others are also ready to return. She checks out the family that she is considering being born into. Will they help in her spiritual development, the lessons she wants to learn, and will she meet with those with whom she wants to work out karmic issues? At some point she goes to the computer room and is matched with the appropriate body and circumstances for the return in which she can make the most progress (Cannon 228-39).

The circumstances that have been decided upon might not be easy, of course. A past life connection might explain our taking an inexplicable and immediate like (or dislike) toward another person. Or explain, the difficult time a child might have with a sibling who, for example, murdered him in a past life. (The story of a friend of mine!) Now is their big chance to learn to accept each other and learn to get along and maybe even to love. On a personal note, a psychic once told me that a current difficult relative had abused me in other lifetimes—as a father and as a brother but now, she assured me, the karma is balanced and the pattern is finished.

Browne (and only she as far as I've read) proposes that our contract includes five Exit Points in case life is too hard and we want to bail out. These options might include such things as a terminal illness or an auto accident. They are potential exit points that we subconsciously may choose to take—or not— in this lifetime. She notes, however, that suicide "is never, ever one of our exit point choices!" (205)

All of this planning might feel like a person's life is predestined. But if so, it's what she herself has predestined, if you will. The spirit guides (masters and teachers) are *guides*, not dictators. The earth, for better or worse, is a planet of Free Will—which means that our best laid plans can go astray. The person, once in the physical, of course does not remember what she decided on the other side—and may not choose to work her plan. As Browne says, "A charted life is in no way a life without options. It exemplifies the fact that the value of our lives isn't dictated by what we're confronted with but by what we do with what we're confronted with" (209).

After the decisions have been made, the person then goes again to the *resting place* in preparation for his re-entry into a physical life—just as he probably went to the resting place during his transition into the astral world.

Apparently re-entry is not fun for the spirit. The womb is cramped and dark. There are reports that the spirit does not have to enter the fetus at conception, but might choose to wait until the birth—and then all those bright lights are a shock! One person in trance reported that the spirit could safely leave the sleeping infant from time to time. If we've read Wordsworth's "Ode on Intimations of Immortality" and take seriously a child who says such things as "I liked my other mother better!", we might suspect that children often remain close to the spirit realm and even their past life (Ramacharaka 166).

What Shall Come Hereafter

Part II

What Shall Come Hereafter

CHAPTER 1

Supporting the Dying

The little unremembered acts of kindness and love are the best of a good man's life.
—William Wordsworth

Most of us feel powerless sitting beside the bed of someone dying. These suggestions may give you some ideas and more confidence in your ability to support your loved one.

- Be fully present. Allow for silence/sacred space. This is their time; honor it.
- In the silence, send them love and peace/reassurance from your heart.
- To connect at an energy level, match your in-breath and out-breath to theirs.

What Shall Come Hereafter

- Touch them with *both* hands—it makes a circle with your heart.
- Be absolutely sincere. Be open to sharing the truth of their situation—they usually intuitively know it though they may not wish to discuss it.
- If you know them well, tell them the story of their life and all the good they've done. Acknowledge the kindness and caring they've shown.
- Ask questions to encourage their story; hear them with compassion and without judgment.
- If they wish, explore their belief system. *Don't try to convert them to yours.*
- Read any spiritual material that resonates with them.
- Assure them that you will continue to pray for and remember them.
- If they are in pain, suggest that they send love and gratitude to the painful area; the fear that often comes with pain results in tightness and resistance; love opens, relaxes and eases pain.
- If they share their fear around dying, give them hope. If they ask for information, and

ONLY then, share your knowledge of what happens when we die.

- If the person is afraid, suggest they ask their God to help them, save them. Offer to pray for them. If it seems apropos, remind them of the verse "Whoever calls upon the name of the Lord shall be saved" (Acts 2:21). This was exactly Howard Storm's cry in his NDE described in *My Descent into Death*, "Jesus, save me!"
- If they share unresolved issues (feelings of anger, remorse or guilt), listen to them. Do not minimize their feelings. In a certain sense, you are acting as their confessor—and with their true repentance, you can assure them of forgiveness.
- The life review/judgment in the astral world will presumably be easier if the person takes care of any guilt over things done or said (or left undone/unsaid) before leaving this life.

Emotional Freedom Techniques offers a simple forgiveness protocol—for both the self and/or another person:

What Shall Come Hereafter

"I forgive myself for _____. I did the very best I could given the circumstances and my spiritual development at that time." Said three times with the hand on the heart.

"I forgive _____ for _____. S/He did the very best s/he could given the circumstances and his/her spiritual development at that time." Said three times with the hand on the heart.

This EFT protocol reminds me of Christ's words on the cross: "Father, forgive them *for they know not what they do.*"

Both the Buddhist and Hindu traditions encourage the person leaving their physical body to keep calm and focused—which is easier, of course, if they have had a spiritual practice in life. The best way I know to keep calm is to pray or meditate by focusing on breathing. You can help them.

CHAPTER 2

Taking Care of the Dead

To the born sure is death, to the dead sure is birth; so for an issue that cannot be escaped thou dost not well to sorrow.
  –*Ellis Peters,* Death to the Landlords

The Jewish tradition, in my opinion, wonderfully supports the newly dead and our own grief process. In Orthodoxy, the body is never left alone before the funeral. Furthermore, it is recommended to stay with the body at least the first 24 hours after the death if possible because the person has not usually yet crossed over. Note that during the dying process and after death, the person is highly clairvoyant; this state can last from 21 to 49 days so it's very important what we say to and about him/her during that period.

What Shall Come Hereafter

The end of the Jewish funeral marks the beginning of an intense mourning period of 7 days (*shiva*/7) during which the bereaved withdraw from public obligations. Mourners sit on low stools and read Psalms, recite prayers and remember the deceased. The community brings food to the bereaved, especially on the first day. For the next 30 days (*sheloshim/30)*, mourners may return to work, but don't participate in entertainments (Pilkington 101).

John O'Donohue, speaking from the Celtic tradition, shares this:

> The soul does not leave the body abruptly.... It is very important not to leave the dead person on his own.... If at all possible, when the person dies, they should be left in their familiar surroundings so that they can make this deeper transition in a comfortable, easy and secure way. The first few weeks after a person dies, that person's soul and memory should be minded and protected. One should say many prayers for the deceased to help the person make the journey home. (214)

D'Anne Olsen

Deborah King likewise tells us that especially within 21 days of the death, your thoughts can impact the person's journey. "Chanting, praying, reading sacred texts, and performing other rituals to help your loved ones in the afterlife can greatly benefit them" (140).

Conservative Protestants are dissuaded from praying for the dead. But they do encourage a sort of death watch—a time to say goodbye to their loved one and to be there to support family members and close friends. There is normally a visitation time of one or two days at a funeral home with a closed or open casket. After the funeral, there is a procession to the grave site where prayers are said and a handful of earth is tossed onto the casket.

Roman Catholics observe three rites: a vigil or wake followed by a funeral liturgy and then by interment. It is common to have a special Mass said for the dead. On Nov 2nd, All Souls Day, all dead are remembered with prayers, meditation and reflection (Berkson 81-2).

Tibetan Buddhism advocates sacred reading to the person as she's dying—and immediately afterwards to alleviate any fear and confusion she might be experiencing if she doesn't know she's dead. This tradition stresses the importance of sacred readings and prayers for the dead for the 21 to 49 days after the death because that's how long it is before the person's rebirth. The first 21 days are especially important. One can pray by visualizing brilliant rays of light pouring down upon them from their sacred being purifying them and freeing them of all confusion and pain, and granting them deep peace. One continues by seeing them taken up into that light, healed now of all negativity and suffering (Rinpoche 302).

In Islam, the dead are buried virtually immediately, that same day if possible. After a ritual bathing, the corpse is wrapped in a simple shroud. The funeral service is said in the presence of the dead who is then carried in procession and buried. There are then three days of official mourning. The mourning should not be excessive—one is encouraged to accept the will of Allah. Forty days after the burial there is a set time for more prayers and the reading of the Qur'an (Berkson 88-9).

In Hinduism, after the death (and the same day if possible), the body is washed, wrapped, adorned with flowers and anointed with sandalwood paste. It is then carried on a stretcher to the place of cremation by a procession of people chanting mantras. After the cremation, the mourners bathe in the river and then share in a ritual feast (Berkson 98-9).

The Egyptians certainly held that the dead needed looking after. They built a mortuary temple for their pharaohs, a place to leave food offerings and say prayers.

CHAPTER 3

Easing Your Grief

*Give sorrow words; the grief that does not speak
Whispers the o'er-fraught heart and bids it break.*
—Macbeth

Grief is a response to many losses: a loved one, a job, a home, a pet, a dream, our health. If we don't grieve all our losses, they'll poison our life.

Some do's and don'ts.

Note that loss, especially sudden and unexpected loss (death of a child, murder, accident, miscarriage, suicide), is usually more devastating than loss from a prolonged illness. Loss of someone from whom you were estranged is also very difficult.

D'Anne Olsen

I was estranged from my father when he died. How I wish I'd known then the exercise below that I share with you.

Estrangement (blocked communication) is often caused by hurt. In a sense, it is unfinished business. Rinpoche in *The Tibetan Book of Living and Dying* offers this exercise:

- Visualize the person in front of you exactly as you knew him/her.
- Then visualize him sitting before you in his new state of awareness and openness—totally willing to share honestly and resolve the problem between you.
- Feel deeply what you want to say—maybe write it down. Then tell the person what the problem is, all your feelings, your difficulties, your hurt, your anger, your regret—everything that you haven't felt safe or comfortable to say before.
- When you have finished, immediately begin to write what he might say in response to you—in his new state of awareness and openness.

Don't think, just write what comes spontaneously, allowing the person to express his side of the problem.
- Search if there is anything else you've forgotten to say; write it down and tell the person. Then, again, listen for and write the other person's response. Continue until there is nothing more to be said or heard.
- Conclude by forgiving the person (and yourself—you both did the best you could under the circumstances). Ask and receive their forgiveness in return.
- Finally, express love and appreciation.
- Then visualize the person turning away and leaving. Even though you let go of the person, keep their love and warm memories in your heart (181-2).

Be extra kind and gentle with yourself. And remember that grief in itself is exhausting. Be realistic about your expectations for yourself. Ask for and accept help—people want to help.

If possible, give yourself a week to do nothing but mourn. Do not hold back tears. They are a huge release. And then very gradually begin to pick up the most important activities of your life. Do something special for yourself. Make plans that have nothing to do with your loss.

Talk out your grief and your memories both to the dead and to others. It is very healing for you to tell the story of his/her life—especially in a group of folks who knew him. You will cry and laugh together. *Do not isolate!*

If your belief system allows it, pray for the dead with all sincerity and love. Talk to them. Tell them how much they meant to you, how much good they have done—and that you will never forget them. At the same time, encourage your loved one to take care of himself and move on. *This not only helps him, but helps you by shifting your focus from yourself to your loved one.*

Read spiritual material. Ask your God or your angels to support and guide you. (Earth is a planet of Free Will. Apparently our spiritual helpers *are not allowed to help us unless we ask.* Recall all the admonitions in the Bible to ask for what we need.) A candle is wonderful for focus. For some it is a reminder of the surrounding presence of the divine.

What Shall Come Hereafter

Do not be distraught and helpless with grief. Or long for the dead to return and be with you. This does your loved one a great disservice because it disturbs him and keeps him connected to the earth plane—preventing him from getting on with his life on the other side.

Dolores Cannon recorded what one spirit said,

> Every time you grieve for someone who is gone, you tie that person a little closer to being earthbound. Grief has its place, but excessive grieving is bad for both the person who is doing the grieving, and the one they are grieving for. There is no reason to grieve for that person. Most of them are very happy where they are. (172- 3)

Honor your loved one—and in the process ease your own grief—by taking action, *choosing to live more intensely on their behalf.* Give to charities they supported, donate their items where they might wish. Imagine fulfilling their aspirations in some way. Do art work, music, writing with them in mind.

Do not quarrel over possessions. Most traditions propose that the veil between the living and the dead is very thin—especially during the first 21-49 days—and the dead can see/hear you.

In Jewish custom, on the evening preceding the anniversary *(yahrzeit)* of the death, a candle is lit which burns for 24 hours—it is a time of reflection.

Though I myself am not Jewish, I find observing the *yahrzeit* for people I love a very important ritual. I remember one morning years ago now, while working on the computer I felt physically that something was wrong, but didn't know what. When I happened to look at a calendar, I realized that it was the one-year anniversary of my stepson's suicide. My body remembered.

If your bereavement is deeper and continues longer than you think it should, ask yourself if at a subconscious level you are holding on to your grief because you think that is the only way to stay close to your loved one. Actually, the opposite seems to be true. C.S. Lewis, *A Grief Observed*, felt closer to his wife when he grieved her less.

Again, bereavement is a process, not a state of being. If the grief doesn't *move*, as a therapist I suspect unresolved (and unnecessary) negative emotional issues. Note that it is *normal* to feel

- shock at the news
- denial
- anger at the deceased for leaving you
- anger at yourself
- resentment
- profound regret
- guilt
- fear for the future
- helplessness and hopelessness.

But these emotions are neither helpful to you *nor to the deceased*. It is my experience that in most cases these unresolved negative emotions can be easily eliminated with EFT and substituted with life-giving healthy ones. Seek help—when you're ready.

Sylvia Browne, commenting on the funeral service, notes that "departed spirits can find themselves deeply torn at the sight of their loved ones in so much pain, so the more joyful and celebratory the service, the easier it is for the deceased to move on in peace" (69).

CHAPTER 4

Supporting the Bereaved

He hath sent me to bind up the brokenhearted...and to comfort all that mourn.
                              –Isaiah 61: 1-2

Supporting another's grief—some do's and don'ts.

Remember that you are there to support so take your clue from the bereaved, of course, but you might consider these general common guidelines.

Be there. Your presence tells the person s/he is not alone. And listening is much more important than speaking. A touch with both hands makes a circle with your heart and communicates caring. Let the person cry.

Listen, listen, listen. Talking is healing. Let them talk whether or not it makes sense to you. Get them to tell you the story of their loved one's life—all the memories.

Don't ask them how they are, but how they are *today.*

Do not give advice unless specifically requested and, even then, be very careful. Do not tell the bereaved that their loved one is in a better place—or try to comfort by telling them that the deceased lived a long life.

Don't tell them you know how they feel—you don't.

If their belief system allows, remind them that spiritual beings are around them—but they must *ask* for help.

People in grief tend to forget about food. Find out when they ate last and what they feel like eating. Bring healthful food that you know they enjoy.

Ask how you can help. Maybe do the laundry, open the mail, do the dishes, get groceries—but be sure they know and want whatever help you offer.

Support decision-making. Mourners tend to be depressed and not clear-thinking. Encourage them to postpone making important decisions as long as possible. Maybe advocate for a spokesperson.

Pay attention. If you think they're in despair or at risk, they may well be. Note that auto accidents and suicides happen more frequently during the grieving process.

Wait to help remove possessions, but if the person is rejecting putting away reminders after what seems a reasonable time, it may be a sign of deeper problems and you may want to encourage her to see a therapist.

CHAPTER 5

How Should We Then Live?

The true saint goes in and out amongst the people and eats and sleeps with them and buys and sells in the market and marries and takes part in social intercourse, and never forgets God for a single moment.

–Abu Sa'id

I've written from various sources what happens after we die and offered suggestions of how to support the bereaved. In the light of this information, I challenge you to think about how to incorporate into your own life the ideas that have resonated with you.

May I propose that your life at every stage is important and meaningful, that you recognize that you have a purpose, a specific task that you and no one else can accomplish. I quote Thoreau's wish "to live deliberately… and not when I came to die, discover that I had not lived."

All religions stress the importance of being *kind*; they tell us that our purpose here is to *love* and *serve others*. The Dalai Lama emphasizes *compassion and altruism.* In Christianity, the Great Commandment is "Love the Lord your God with all your heart and with all your soul and love your neighbor as yourself." Matt. 22:37-8 It is my belief that it is never too late to become more loving and to begin working out the specific way we can fulfill our purpose.

But at the same time, as Deborah King says, "Caring about the needs of others…doesn't negate the need to be kind to yourself…. Remember that by taking care of yourself, you'll be constantly filling your well so that you'll always have something to give to others" (162).

I believe we should strive to live thankfully, joyfully, fearlessly and fully—more and more in the *present*. People diagnosed with terminal illnesses do this better than most. My favorite books on this topic are Eckhart Tolle's *The Power of Now* and Thich Nhat Hanh's *The Miracle of Mindfulness*. And when life is difficult, I try to remember the AA sayings each of which begins with "Just for Today". I especially like "Just for Today,

I will try to live through this day only". And "Just for Today, I will be happy".

You know the saying, "Today is the first day of the rest of your life." In a certain sense, today is the *only* day of the rest of your life. When tomorrow comes, it is today.

Our spiritual teachers tell us to live in the awareness of the eternal—striving to move toward the *spiritual* and away from the *ego-centric and material* dimension. They suggest having a spiritual practice of sacred reading, regular prayer and meditation. At its most basic, meditation is simply focusing on one thing; it could be a focus on the breath or a word or sound—OM, for example. (There are many books and classes available to help you learn how to meditate.) The great guide for me continues to be Brother Lawrence's little book, *The Practice of the Presence of God*.

Tibetan Buddhism speaks of the importance of letting go of our fear of death: fear of pain, of indignity, of dependence, of losing control, fear of separation, fear that our life has been meaningless and "perhaps our greatest fear of all is fear of fear itself, which grows more powerful the more we evade it" (Rinpoche 180). That tradition stresses the importance of dying *consciously*, being fully aware of every moment not only in life but also in death (Berkson 102-05).

Islam encourages us to live better by being aware of our own death even in daily life. A suggested practice time is before sleep—by laying on the right side (as in the grave)—realizing one might die that night (Berkson 90).

King stresses working on ourselves *now*—while we are still in the physical. She suggests (as the ancients said) Know Thyself, be aware of "your basest negative emotions and thought patterns—your jealousy fear, anger, resentment, self-pity, entitlement, selfishness and narcissism" (143). Admit your failings and then move on from feeling 'not good enough'—self-rejection—to self-forgiveness. Remember that the judgment after death is, by all accounts, a self judgment. (I'd like to think we can review our life and forgive ourselves ahead of time.)

The Roman Catholic Church is very helpful around this because it offers Confession, a chance to examine one's attitude/behavior while there is still time. Ideally a person comes away accepting divine forgiveness (and self-forgiveness) and with a determination to live better.

What Shall Come Hereafter

Always the English professor, I note my favorite play, "King Lear," the great story of transformation. The king, formerly the poster boy for narcissism, during the storm begins to think of others. Outside the hovel, he says to his fool, "In boy, go *first*." And he realizes how he'd neglected his kingdom. "Oh, I have ta'en too little care of this!" At the end of his life (Act IV, vii) Lear, the king, *kneels* before his daughter and begs her forgiveness. And dies shortly thereafter.

In the past I have said that I want a "good death" by which I meant dying easily in my sleep. Now I know that dying like that doesn't give a person the chance to make important choices and perhaps grow spiritually. Even those dying a slow and painful death can take advantage of palliative medications and use the time as an opportunity to take care of any unfinished business and express love, appreciation and even forgiveness to those surrounding them.

And finally, practically speaking, *always be prepared*: have an Advanced Directive, a Durable Power of Attorney for Health Care, a Revocable Living Trust, an up-to-date Will, a Durable Financial Power of Attorney. Some folks also like to make out an Ethical Will in which one can share any important thoughts, beliefs, values, any messages to those one is leaving behind.

If you do not change direction, you may end up where you are heading.
–Lao Tzu

What Shall Come Hereafter

APPENDIX

Yogi Ramacharaka on Spiritual Development

Yoga philosophy teaches that man has always lived and always will live.

That death is but a falling to sleep to awaken in the morning.

That life is continuous, and that its object is development, growth, unfoldment.

That we are in eternity now as much as we ever can be.

That the soul is the real person, not merely an appendage to his physical body.

That as we live out the experiences of one earth life, we pass out of the body into a state of rest, and after that are reborn into bodies and into conditions in accordance with our needs and desires.

That the real life is really a succession of lives—our present self being the result of the experiences gained in our previous existences.

That the universe is great and large, and that there are countless worlds and spheres for its inhabitants, and that we shall not be bound to earth one moment after we are fitted to move to higher spheres and planes.

That those souls who have traveled over the path which we are now treading—our elder brothers—are constantly giving us their aid and encouragement, and are often extending to us a helping hand although we don't recognize it.(Ramacharaka 230-32)

Swami Vishnudevananda on the Sheaths of the Body

Yogis recognize a total of five sheaths divided into three bodies: 1) the Physical Body, 2) the Astral Body and 3) the Causal/Spiritual Body. Most of us are only aware of the first and most dense, the Physical Body. These other bodies/layers of energy/sheaths (the Astral Body) are visible in Kirlian photography and to some psychics as the human aura. The aura appears in various colors because the layers vibrate at different speeds—think of our color spectrum.

The first layer of the Astral Body is known as the *Vital Sheath*, also referred to as the *Etheric Body* or *Etheric Double*. It is an exact replica of the physical body though of a finer substance. It supplies energy to the physical body at the energy vortices or *chakras*. (This energy sheath includes our persistent positive and negative thoughts and emotions—*which eventually manifest in health or disease in the physical body*.) The etheric body is attached to the physical body by a silver cord; when that cord is severed, the person has crossed over and the physical body dies. It is this astral layer (sometimes seen as a ghost) which can leave the body during the sleep/dream state and during meditation and deep trance—which explains accounts of some advanced persons bi-locating, that is, appearing in two places at once.

According to Yoga philosophy, the second and third sheaths of the Astral Body are the Emotional sheath and the Mental sheath respectively. The Causal/Spiritual Body is covered by the Blissful sheath.

SwamiVishnudevananda (12-20) as well as James Van Praagh (28-32).

Sylvia Browne's "Seven Levels of Advancement in the Afterworld"

Level 1. Reentry to The Other Side, reunion with loved ones and the life review (Scanning Machine).

Level 2. Orientation process for the newly arrived—which might involve Soul Slumber (Cocooning).

Level 3. The physical and science skills—theoretical and hands-on vocations.

Level 4. The creative arts: music, writing, painting, theatre.

Level 5. "Research, in which all areas of progress are explored and passed on to earth through infused knowledge."

Level 6. "The teachers, Orientators, lecturers and seminar leaders."

Level 7. The level in which a spirit gives up individual identity and is absorbed into "the

What Shall Come Hereafter

infinite, unfathomable force field from which the love and power of God emanate" (180-1).

Cannon's Spirit Guide's "Levels of Existence"

A person in spirit (between lives) delineated to Cannon these levels of *existence*—which include the earth as well as Browne's levels of advancement in the *afterworld*. Note similarities.

Level 1. Elementals. The plane of pure emotions and energies. These are powerful life forms but without personality.

Level 2. These are the guides and guardians of the plant and animal world. Nature spirits. The Greeks called them sprites or driads. They are our "little people," fairies or leprechauns and the devas contacted in *Findhorn Garden*. They belong to the spirit realm but can manifest physically.

Level 3. Animals and a very few people without conscience or intelligence.

Level 4. Humans with intelligence but no conscience: sociopaths, murderers and criminals.

Level 5. The earth, "your day-to-day existence."

Level 6. The spirit realm and the realm of ghosts—those choosing the earth and those kept there by their family's grief, for example. Also called the Lower Astral.

Level 7. The schools of knowledge and thought. An inventor or musician might have access to this level—and not know where the information comes from.

Levels 8 and 9. Reserved for the great masters who no longer need to incarnate but may in order to help humanity. Jesus, said Suddi in *Jesus and the Essenes,* was on the 9th level, almost to the 10th.

Level 10. Oneness with God.

Cannon's spirit guide noted that these levels are not fixed. You'll remember (the chapter on the Nature of the Afterworld) that the spiritual planes are all around us, but each is vibrating at a different frequency—and can be accessed in meditation, dream, trance or during an NDE (88-109).

A.M.H. Atwater (*Near-Death Experiences*) hints at the same when he said that the following historical figures all had NDEs as children which gave them more access to the spiritual world: "Einstein, Abraham Lincoln, Queen Elizabeth I, Edward de Vere (the 17th Earl of Oxford and believed by many to be the real Shakespeare), Winston Churchill, Black Elk, Walter Russell, Valerie V. Hunt—plus most of the saints in the Catholic Church" (51).

What Shall Come Hereafter

FAVORITE PRAYERS, AFFIRMATIONS AND QUOTATIONS

Heal me where I am in the deepest need of healing.
Grant that I might serve you with my life.
Give me all that I need in order to do your will.
Help me to become an effective instrument
of your healing power.
—Jack Miller

ಚಲಚಲ

You who are the source of all power,
whose rays illuminate the world,
Illuminate also my heart
so that it too can do your work.
—Author unknown

ಚಲಚಲ

It is the Lord who goes before you. He will be with
you; He will not leave you nor forsake you.
Do not fear or be dismayed.
—Deut. 31:8

ಚಲಚಲ

What Shall Come Hereafter

*The grace of God is a wind
which is always blowing.*
—Sri Ramakrishna

☙❧

*For surely I know the plans I have for you,
says the Lord,
plans for your welfare and not for harm,
to give you a future with hope.
Then when you call upon me
and come and pray to me,
I will hear you.
When you search for me, you will find me;
if you seek me with all your heart,
I will let you find me.
I will restore all your fortunes and
I will bring you back.*
—Jer. 29: 11-14

☙❧

*On this plane of free will, everything counts.
Each decision either raises you up energetically
or lowers your vibration.
Each decision is a deal with the dark
or with the light. Nothing is neutral.*
—Deborah King

☙❧

D'Anne Olsen

*I choose by all my God-given brilliance
to shine out into the world
for the highest good of all
—a light to heal, transform, inspire.
I let go of the "how's" and "when's"
and focus on giving my gifts at the highest level.
I allow divine guidance to lead me to fulfill
my highest purpose—suited to my abilities and joy.
I am guided, blessed, safe, abundant.
The steps will appear just as I need them.
I joyously anticipate what is on its way to me.*
–Margaret Lynch

ଔଔ

*The right people are coming into my life
who can help me and make me happy
and who I can help and make happy.
Those who are not for my highest good
fade out of my life—and find their good elsewhere.
I walk in the circle of God's love
and am divinely irresistible
to my greatest good now.*
–Author unknown

ଔଔ

What Shall Come Hereafter

*Even at this moment the universe is orchestrating
easy doors for me to open and
abundant supply for all I need and want.*
	—Carol James

ଓଓ

*Nothing will change for the better
until I change for the better.*
	—Hardy Margosian

ଓଓ

*All is well.
Everything is working out to my highest good.
Out of this situation only good will come.
I am safe—and divinely guided.*
	—Louse Hay

ଓଓ

That which we hold in consciousness will be made manifest for us; therefore we should not hold the thought of anything that we do not want to see appear.

	—Charles Fillmore

ଓଓ

D'Anne Olsen

*All that has offended me, I forgive.
Whatever has made me bitter, resentful, unhappy,
I forgive.
Within and without, I forgive.
Things past, things present, things future, I forgive.*
　　　　　　　　　　　　–Author unknown

ॐ

*To love means loving the unlovable,
To forgive means pardoning the unpardonable,
Faith means believing the unbelievable,
Hope means hoping when everything is hopeless.*
　　　　　　　　　　　　–G.K. Chesterton

ॐ

*Forgiving moves us from being a victim
to being in charge.*
　　　　　　　　　–James Van Praagh

ॐ

*Love is the law of God.
You live that you may learn to love.
You love that you may learn to live.
No other lesson is required of man.*
　　　　　　　　　　　　–Mikhail Naimy

ॐ

What Shall Come Hereafter

*I let go my tense hold
on persons, places, events and things.
I let go what goes.
I am not afraid to let go of possessive attitudes
toward my dear ones or toward my possessions,
for I know what a person humanly releases
she never loses.
It is only what which she tries to tensely possess
that slips though her closed fingers and escapes her.
That which I willingly surrender I never lose:
that or something better will always be given me.
Release produces perfect results of health, wealth
and happiness for me and through me now.*
—Author unknown

ಚಚ

*He that cannot forgive others breaks the bridge
over which he must pass himself,
for every man has need to be forgiven.*
—Thomas Fuller

ಚಚ

*Your higher self is powerful beyond measure,
and the light of who you are is worth sharing
with the world.
You can make a difference!*
—Deborah King

D'Anne Olsen

*God, grant me the serenity
to accept the things I cannot change.
Courage to change the things I can.
And the wisdom to know the difference.*
—Reinhold Niebuhr

ଔଔ

*O Lord, how entirely needful is thy grace for me,
to begin any good work,
to go on with it, and to accomplish it.
For without that grace I can do nothing;
but in thee I can do all things
when thy grace doth strengthen me.*
—Thomas A. Kempis

ଔଔ

*If the only prayer you ever say in your entire life
is thank you, it will be enough.*
—Meister Eckhart

ଔଔ

*Write it on your heart
that every day is the best day of the year.*
—Ralph Waldo Emerson

What Shall Come Hereafter

BIBLIOGRAPHY

Atwater, P.M.H. *Near-Death Experiences: the Rest of the Story*. New York: MJF Books, 2011.

Berkson, Mark, PhD. *Death, Dying, and the Afterlife: Lessons from World Cultures*. Chantilly, Virginia: The Great Courses, 2016.

Browne, Sylvia with Lindsay Harrison. *Life on the Other Side: A Psychic's Tour of the Afterlife*. New York: a Signet Book, 2001.

Cannon, Delores. *Between Death and Life: Conversations with a Spirit*. Huntsville: Ozark Mountain Publishers, 1993.

Cannon, Dolores. *Jesus and the Essenes*. Huntsville: Ozark Mountain Publishers, 1992.

King, Deborah. *Entangled in Darkness: Seeking the Light*. New York: Hay House, 2013.

Moody, Raymond A. Jr., M.D. with Paul Perry. *Paranormal: My Life in Pursuit of the Afterlife*. New York: HarperCollins, 2012.

O'Donohue, John. *Anam Cara: A Book of Celtic Wisdom*. New York: HarperCollins, 1998.

Parti, Rajiv, M.D. with Paul Perry. *Dying to Wake Up: A Doctor's Voyage into the Afterlife and the Wisdom He Brought Back*. New York: Atria Books, 2016.

Parnia, Sam, M.D. with Josh Young. *Erasing Death: The Science that is Rewriting the Boundaries between Life and Death*. New York: HarperCollins, 2013.

Pilkington, C.M. *Judaism*. Teach Yourself Books. Chicago: NTC Publishing Group, 1995.

Plato. *Six Great Dialogues: Apology, Crito, Phaedo, Phaedrus, Symposium, The Republic*. New York: Dover Publishers, 2007.

Rinpoche, Sogyal. *The Tibetan Book of Living and Dying*. San Francisco: Harper, 1994.

Ritchie, George G., M.D. with Elizabeth Sherrill. *Return from Tomorrow*. Grand Rapids: Baker Book House, 1978.

Steinsaltz, Adin. *The Thirteen Petalled Rose: A Discourse on the Essence of Jewish Existence and Belief.* New York: Basic Books, Inc., 1980.

Storm, Howard. *My Descent into Death: A Second Chance at Life.* New York, Doubleday, 2005.

Swami Vishudevananda. *The Complete Illustrated Book of Yoga.* New York: Pocket Books, 1972.

The Bible, Authorized King James Version, New York: Oxford UP, 1909.

Van Praagh, James. *Reaching Heaven: A Spiritual Journey through Life and Death.* New York: Dutton, 1999.

Weiss, Brian L., M.D. *Through Time into Healing.* New York: Simon & Schuster, 1992.

Yogi Ramacharaka. *The Life Beyond Death.* Chicago: Yogi Publication Society, 1909.

I've read many other books, but they either repeat information included in the above or don't add anything apropos to this particular discussion.

What Shall Come Hereafter

RECOMMENDED READING

Cannon, Delores. *Between Death and Life: Conversations with a Spirit*. Huntsville: Ozark Mountain Publishers, 1993.

Cannon reports the between-life accounts of many, many spirits in her hypnotic regression sessions. She includes topics not covered in this book.

Cannon, Dolores. *Jesus and the Essenes*. Huntsville: Ozark Mountain Publishers, 1992.

I especially like this past life regression record because (in my belief system) it is not only an eye witness account of Qumran (the amazing community that wrote and hid the Dead Sea Scrolls), but is also an eye witness account of Jesus' birth, ministry, death and resurrection.

Easwaran, Eknath. *Words to Live By: Inspiration for Every Day*. Tomales, CA: The Blue Mountain Center of Mediatation, 1990.

This was one of my pastor Bob Flaherty's daily readings and now one of my own. Delightfully nonsectarian.

Gawande, Atul. *Being Mortal: Medicine and What Matters in the End*. New York: Metropolitan Books, 2014.
In my opinion, a must-read for anyone working in end-of-life care.

King, Deborah. *Entangled in Darkness: Seeking the Light*. New York: Hay House, 2013.
This is the most important book I've ever read on spiritual growth and healing. A must for therapists.

O'Donohue, John. *Anam Cara: A Book of Celtic Wisdom*. New York: HarperCollins, 1998.
O'Donohue, priest and poet, includes aging and death in his discussion of Celtic wisdom. His Irish prose is as nourishing for me as his wisdom.

Ritchie, George G., M.D. with Elizabeth Sherrill. *Return from Tomorrow*. Grand Rapids: Baker Book House, 1978.

D'Anne Olsen

One of the first and most inclusive of near-death experience accounts. Ritchie's story has forever challenged the working out of my own spiritual life.

Storm, Howard. *My Descent into Death: A Second Chance at Life*. New York, Doubleday, 2005.

His NDE and subsequent life change initially horrified and then inspired me.

Weiss, Brian L., M.D. *Many Lives, Many Masters*. New York: Simon & Schuster, 1988.

Written by a psychiatrist whose belief system did not initially include past lives. A great first read on reincarnation and between-lives messages.

Yogi Ramacharaka. *The Life Beyond Death*. Chicago: Yogi Publication Society, 1909.

If one reads only two books on the Afterlife, I recommend this along with Dolores Cannon's *Between Life and Death*.

What Shall Come Hereafter

ACKNOWLEDGEMENTS

I'm very grateful not only for the many, many authors that have been part of my investigation of the Afterworld, but also for all my good angels and encouragers: Doreen Pittman, Jackie Lane, Richard Gratz, Bob Flaherty, Danette O'Quin, Karen Matte, Bernadine Veiga, Joelle McCormick, and my brother Ernie Olsen—to name only a few. To all who have walked so faithfully beside me, thank you.

What Shall Come Hereafter

ABOUT THE AUTHOR

D'Anne Olsen is a person of many passions. After earning her PhD in Literature and teaching English in numerous colleges, she realized that her real purpose in life was to be a helper/ healer/supporter. Following her teaching career, she worked in social services, trained as a Yoga instructor, was licensed as a massage therapist and eventually as an Emotional Freedom Techniques (EFT tapping) practitioner. Her work as a therapist led to her writing *Return to Joy*, a short EFT book for those struggling with depression. Though she spent much of her adult life reading about Hamlet's "what shall come hereafter," she never dreamed that one day she'd choose to share those surprises with others on the journey.

She can be reached at 1.971.506.0498 and daolsen711@hotmail.com www.EFTLiveYourDream.

www.ingramcontent.com/pod-product-compliance
Lightning Source LLC
Chambersburg PA
CBHW060329050426
42449CB00011B/2706